A Prayer From the Heart

O God, our Father, we want to thank You
for being everywhere!
We thank You for your long patience
while waiting at the door of our hearts
with blessings to share with us.
Our hope is in You alone:
nourish and fortify our hope.
Grant us strength and courage, day by day,
to be willing servants of Christ, our Redeemer.
O Christ, in Your love, guide us
from darkness to light,
so to appreciate Your love.
May we banish anxiety,
by trusting and reflecting on Your faithfulness.
Teach us patience in our relationships
with our fellow human beings.
May the pure wind of the Holy Spirit
blow away the haze of ignorance,
and the mist of prejudice,
that we may see clearly
what You would have us see.
Lift our eyes from our worldly interests,
to see the sufficiency of Your love
for all our needs, in Christ's name.

The Footprints Book of Prayers

Also by Margaret Fishback Powers, available from HarperCollins Publishers Ltd:

Footprints: The True Story Behind The Poem
Footprints: Gift Edition
Life's Little Inspiration Book
A Heart for Children

The Footprints Book of Prayers

Margaret Fishback Powers

HarperCollins*PublishersLtd*

First published in the U.K. by Marshall Pickering, an Imprint of
HarperCollins Religious, part of HarperCollins Publishers: 1996

First edition

Canadian Cataloguing in Publication Data

Powers, Margaret Fishback
The footprints book of prayers

ISBN 0-00-255398-8

1. Prayers.   2. Devotional literature.
I. Title.

BV245.P68 1996   242   C95-932449-6

96 97 98 99 EB 10 9 8 7 6 5 4 3 2 1

Printed and bound in the United States

Footprints

One night I dreamed a dream.
I was walking along the beach with my Lord.
Across the dark sky flashed scenes from my life.
For each scene, I noticed two sets of footprints in the sand,
one belonging to me and one to my Lord.
When the last scene of my life shot before me
I looked back at the footprints in the sand
and to my surprise,
I noticed that many times along the path of my life
there was only one set of footprints.
I realized that this was at the lowest
and saddest times of my life.
This always bothered me
and I questioned the Lord
about my dilemma.
'Lord, you told me when I decided to follow You,
You would walk and talk with me all the way.
But I'm aware that during the most troublesome
times of my life there is only one set of footprints.
I just don't understand why, when I needed You most,
You leave me.'
He whispered, 'My precious child,
I love you and will never leave you
never, ever, during your trials and testings.
When you saw only one set of footprints
it was then that I carried you.'

*To my husband, Paul, who spends
more time in prayer for the ministry
to children than hours in programmes with them.*

Contents

Preface

The rest of my family are still asleep, but I've been awake now since just before 3 a.m. Serenity, my daughter's Maltese, has been barking at the patio doors for some time. It seems that this is when the racoons love to go walking on our fence to our neighbour's garden, and for the last couple of nights it seems my arthritis has chosen the same time schedule to create havoc in my back and right foot. I couldn't get back to sleep, so I decided to get up and pray for a while!

I have discovered the best place for me to pray is at the chair in my writing nook in what we call our 'Upper Room'. As I was praying I realized that I was praying the same usual prayer: 'Heavenly Father, please do this . . . or that . . . for me or someone', and it was getting more repetitious by the moment. These past few nights, my prayers have been like a dripping tap!

My mind wandered back to my Pastor's message from last Sunday, concerning the character of God. He had reminded us that God is a loving, compassionate and caring Father, and yet this prayer time with Him seemed so 'empty' and impersonal. I mused that if my relationship was not right with Him, then it would be reasonable to assume that *I* am not right with Him, *and not vice versa.*

I started thinking (out loud) to my Father in Heaven – not about what I wanted Him to do for the ministry He called our family to, for our home, our church, our children and for me – but about what this compassionate, loving Father had *already* done on the cross in Jesus Christ for so many generations, and what He had done for so many years and was doing *right now* for me personally.

A popular song started to come into my mind, about His watching over us from a distance and I knew that it is not *just* from a distance but that He is here walking beside us and talking with us daily. A feeling overwhelmed me to *thank* God for His wonderful goodness and grace. I asked Him to strengthen my faith anew and to grant me the understanding to trust Him more. There came such a calmness to my feelings. This tenderness was something that I don't think had been there for a long time, or if it had, it seemed as from a dream long ago. I felt both drained and renewed.

I'd like to suggest that the next time you can't sleep, you get up, find a place to kneel in prayer and thank God for what He had done on the cross in love for you! Understand that this Heavenly Father really is caring, compassionate, comforting and concerned. Have faith in His goodness for your life and trust Him with it, then go back to bed and get a good night's rest, secure in the knowledge of His unconditional promises of love for you!

As you take time to pray it is my fervent hope that you will find guideposts of direction in this book of prayers to point you along in those intimate and personal moments with your Heavenly Father. And I will pray for you; would you also pray for me?

Margaret Fishback Powers
July 1995

One

EMMANUEL – GOD WITH US

'One night I dreamed a dream.
I was walking along the beach with my Lord . . .'

One morning at the breakfast table, we were discussing plans for the day. One of our girls made a casual remark: 'I dreamed that we had a maid who could take care of cleaning up my room and doing all the laundry each day.' But as she came to the end of her thoughts, she commented, 'Well, I guess I'll just have to dream on . . . as I make up my bed myself.'

Some of our dreams can have a powerful effect on us. I have on occasions woken up laughing or fretful – and all because of a dream. Not all of our dreams are disappointing, but then again, only a small portion of our wishful thinking dreams ever come true. There are dreams our children have shared with us over the years that have touched us to the very soul. I remember one. Our youngest was in hospital for an operation and she used to start feeling very frightened towards evening. As I left the room one night, I kissed her forehead and said, 'Don't worry, dear. God will send His angels to watch over you.'

When I arrived the next morning, she was sitting up chattering away to a nurse, with her face beaming. Later on, the nurse turned to me and said, 'Your daughter has quite an imagination. She was describing to me the angels that were sitting on the end of her bed, and told me not to be afraid, and that her operation would go all right.' Later, my daughter described that same dream to me . . . giving her angels names. Strangely enough, many years later, as a young woman of eighteen years, these same angels visited her again after she experienced a serious accident. Surely no coincidence!

One of the many names given to Jesus Christ in the Bible is Emmanuel, which means, literally, 'God with us'. What a promise is contained in that name! In Christ, God made His dwelling place with ordinary human beings, and as He was returning to heaven, Jesus gave His disciples another great promise, 'I am with you always, to the very end of the age.' That God is there for us whenever we turn to Him is no pipe-dream!

Jesus Christ has brought every need, every joy, every gratitude, every hope of men before God. He accompanies us, and brings us into the presence of God.

DIETRICH BONHOEFFER

No man cometh unto the Father, but by me. John 14:6

Heavenly Father, I most heartily thank Thee, that it hath pleased Thy fatherly goodness to take care of me this night past. I most entirely beseech Thee, O most merciful Father, to show the like kindness toward me this day, in preserving my body and my soul.

THOMAS BECON 1512–1567

And whatever we ask, we receive from Him. 1 John 3:22

O Lord, Our Lord, how excellent is Thy name in all the earth! Who hast set Thy glory above the heavens. Out of the mouth of babes and sucklings hast Thou ordained strength because of thine enemies, that Thou mightest still the enemy and the avenger.

PSALM 8:1–2

But that ye may know that the Son of man hath power on earth to forgive sins. Matthew 9:6

Lord, God Almighty! Teach me to see things as Christ does and to dream dreams worth telling and following.

P. M. P.

I will pour out my Spirit upon all flesh. Acts 2:17

I know I shall see in His beauty the King in whose law I
  delight,
Who lovingly guards my footsteps and gives me songs in the
  night.

FANNY CROSBY, 1882

Thou wilt hear, O Lord my God. Psalm 38:15

Jesus is all the world to me, my life, my joy, my all;
He is my strength from day to day, without Him I would fall.

W. A. THOMPSON, 1904

[They] will put their trust in Thee. Psalm 9:10

Almighty God, unto whom all hearts are open, all desires
known and from whom no secrets are hid, cleanse the
thoughts of our hearts by the inspiration of Thy Holy Spirit,
that we may love Thee and worthily magnify Thy Holy
Name. Amen.

GREGORY 1

And these words, which I command thee this day, shall be in thine heart. Deuteronomy 6:6

Grant to me, O Lord, to worship Thee in spirit and in truth; help me to open my heart to Thy love and to surrender my will to Thy purpose. Through Jesus Christ my Lord.

M. F. P.

Thou shalt love the Lord thy God with all thy heart, with all thy soul, and with all thy mind. Matthew 22:37

Bless the Lord, O my soul! O Lord my God Thou art very great! . . . O Lord, how manifold are Thy works! In wisdom hast Thou made them all; the earth is full of Thy riches. . . . I will sing praise to my God while I have being. My meditation of Him shall be sweet: I will be glad in the Lord. . . . Bless thou the Lord, O my soul! Praise ye the Lord!

PSALM 104:1, 24,33–34, 35

The Lord is my strength and song, and He is become my salvation: He is my God, and I will prepare Him an habitation: my father's God, and I will exalt Him. Exodus 15:2

Heavenly Father, I recognize my unworthiness to receive any gift from You, especially one as magnificent as eternal salvation through Jesus Christ Your Son. Thank you. May my little life reflect in some way the glory of Your grace.

M. F. P.

But unto every one of us is given grace according to the measure of the gift of Christ. Ephesians 4:7

Eternal God, You are so great and I am so small. Thank you for allowing me to approach Your throne. I rejoice at the greatness of Your grace in placing me in the Saviour and at the constant demonstration of Your kindness to me.

M. F. P.

[We] rejoice in hope of the glory of God. Romans 5:2

Dear God, thank you for coming to us in Your Son and our Saviour, to give us the gift of eternal life, salvation by faith. We know that we now have to make a decision to believe or perish. Making the right decision will assure us to be part of the age to come, the age that never ceases. Thank you, God, for Your wonderful gift that cannot be inherited or earned. It is free!

M. F. P.

He gave His only begotten Son. John 3:16

We realize, God that any approach to you apart from Jesus Christ our Lord is futile. Cults, community or civic groups and various religions can miss the message of Your Word if they talk about You, but do not know You through Your Son. There is *no* approach to You apart from Your Son.

M. F. P.

He that believeth in the Son hath everlasting life. John 3:36

Two

LIGHT IN DARK PLACES

'Across the dark sky flashed scenes from my life . . .'

A few years after Paul and I were married, we were travelling in Tennessee, USA. We decided to take a day trip to visit some caves called 'The Lost Sea'. I am not really into dark caves or narrow tunnels, but joined in on the excursion for the sake of Paul and our friends. We followed the guide through a dark, musty, wet and murky stairwell, past the bare dim light bulbs. Holding on to Paul's hand gave me a bit of extra courage. When we arrived at the Lost Sea and went out in the glass bottom boat, the guide decided it was time for us to get the full impact of the cave, and the lights were turned off, crushing the void into the BLACKEST darkness I have ever experienced. It seemed my heart fairly took off with fear and trembling, and even though my husband had his arms around me, I felt totally alone. Over the years, moments of darkness have come over me – the loss of a friend, the homegoing of a saint, or the great tragedies that occur in the world. However, there is a greater darkness than all this: the darkness I see in a person in whose eyes there is no light of love, who has not felt the rescuing strength of hope, the grace of God in forgiveness, who like Bunyan's traveller seems to cry, 'I'm lost, I'm lost, I'm lost'. There is hope. There is light. He is the light. Jesus Christ, the Son of God, is His name.

O Lord our God, grant me grace to desire You with my whole heart; that so desiring I may seek and find You. So finding You, may love You, and loving You, may hate those sins from which You have redeemed us.

ANSELM 1033–1109

Lord, thou hast heard the desire of the humble: thou wilt prepare their heart . . . Psalm 10:17

Lead us not into temptation, but deliver us from evil. For Thine is the kingdom, the power and the glory for ever and ever, Amen.

THE LORD'S PRAYER

His eyes are open unto their cry. Psalm 34:15

Jesus Thou art waiting, oh, come to Him now, waiting today, waiting today;
Come with our sins, at thy feet lowly bow; Come, and no longer delay.

FANNY CROSBY, 1911

Blessed is that man that maketh the Lord his trust. Psalm 40:4

O Lord Jesus, let Your precious blood be to my soul a
cleansing flood. Turn not, O Lord, this quest away, but grant
that justified I may go to my home at peace with Thee. O
God be merciful to me!

MAGUS LANDSTAD, 1802

*I called upon the Lord in distress: the Lord answered me and set me
in a large place. Psalm 118:6*

Do you need a friend to help you in life's darkest hour?
When you struggle with temptation, feel its deadly power?
There is one above all others, will your cause defend;
You can always count on Jesus, He's my friend.

G. O. WEBSTER, 1916

*The Lord is good, a strong hold in the day of trouble and He
knoweth them that trust in Him. Nahum 1:7*

The Path to the cross, He was willing to tread, all the sins of
my life to forgive.

F. A. BRECK, 1899

*For ask now of the days that are past . . . Unto Thee it was shewed,
that thou mightest know that the Lord He is God. Deuteronomy
4:32, 35*

In sorrow's hour His tender love abideth, for every woe He hath a soothing balm; 'Mid every stormy tempest, wildly beating, He whispers peace, and there is instant calm.

F. A. BRECK, 1909

He giveth power to the faint; and to them that have no might He increaseth strength. Isaiah 40:29

O most Glorious and exalted Lord, You are glorified in the heavens above, yet in Your grace You wished to be glorified by mankind on earth. Free us, Lord, in Your compassion from whatever cares hinder our worship of You, and teach us to seek Your kingdom and its righteousness, may we sing Your praises.

M. F. P.

The Lord knoweth them that are His. 2 Timothy 2:19

Do the waves of trouble rise overwhelming?
Is your sky with tempest overcast?
Flee to God our never failing refuge;
He will shield thee, till the storm is past.

F. KIRKLAND, 1901

Peace, I leave with you, My peace I give unto you. John 14:27

Day by day and with each passing moment, strength I find
to meet my trials here: Trusting in my Father's wise
bestowment, I've no cause for worry or for fear. He whose
heart is kind beyond all measure. Gives unto each day
what He deems best.

CAROLINA SANDELL BERG, 1832

My grace is sufficient for Thee. 2 Corinthians 12:9

I take, O cross, Thy shadow for my abiding place;
I ask no other sunshine than the sunshine of His face;
Content to let the world go by, to know no gain nor loss,
My sinful self my only shame, My glory all the cross.

ELIZABETH CLEPHANE 1830–1869

Now there stood by the cross of Jesus His mother. John 19:25

Our Father in Heaven, thank you for reminding me, I am not
my own but have been bought with a price, with the blood
of Jesus. The world is new to every soul when Christ has
entered into it. Loving Saviour, we can never perish if we
remain in the arms of our Eternal Father.

M. F P.

Thanks be to God which giveth us the victory. 1 Corinthians 15:56

All seeing, gracious Lord, my heart before Thee lies;
All sin of thought and life abhorred, my soul to Thee would
  rise.
Hear Thou my prayer, O God. Unite my heart to Thee;
Beneath Thy love, from sin, deliver me.

REVEREND HENRY GRAVES, 1881

Hear my prayer, O Lord. Psalm 143:1

Sad and weary, lone and dreary,
Lord I would Thy call obey.
Thee believing, Christ receiving,
I would come to Thee today.
Be Thou near me, keep and cheer me,
Thro' life's dark and stormy ways.
Turn my sadness into gladness,
Turn my darkness into day.

A. STARBRIGHT, 1881

Come unto me all ye that labour and are heavy laden. Matthew 11:28

Loving Father, you know the way I take, Oh Lord, You know
the path I climb. Heavenly Father, whatever happens, Thou
will be by my side and never forsake me. If my soul grows
weary You will be my song in the night.

M. F. P.

Bless the Lord, O my soul . . . who redeemeth thy life from destruction.

PSALM 103:2, 4

Jesus, my Lord to Thee I cry, unless Thou help me I would
   die;
Oh, bring Thy free salvation nigh, Helpless I am and full of
   guilt.
But yet for me Thy blood was spilt and Thou can make me
   what Thou will.
Teach me to walk the path you will.

E. H. H., 1881

*Hear my prayer, O Lord, and let my cry come unto Thee. Psalm
102:1*

The way is dark, Heavenly Father, cloud upon cloud is
gathering thickly about my head. Lord, thunder roars above
me; Father, I stand like one bewildered! Dear Father, take my
hand and through the gloom lead safely home Thy child.

M. F. P.

*For the Lord God is a sun and shield: the Lord will give grace and
glory. Psalm 84:11*

Blessed Lord, strengthen our souls with the fullness of Thy divine teaching. Guide us in deep teachings of Thy heavenly wisdom and of Thy great mercy; lead us by Thy Word into everlasting life, through Jesus Christ our Saviour. Amen.

BROOKE WESTCOTT 1825–1901

What things soever ye desire, when ye pray, believe that ye shall receive them, and you shall have them. Mark 11:24

Dear Heavenly Father, I know that darkness comes to all on earth at some time, but help me to see You past the shadows, for I know that in order for there to be shadows there must be a light. Only Your light can bring us out of the darkness. Lord, lead me in Your path by the true light.

P. M. P.

Then spake Jesus again unto them, saying, 'I am the Light of the world.' John 8:12

To pray is to let Jesus into our lives. He knocks and seeks admittance, not only in the solemn hours of secret prayer, He knocks in the midst of your daily work, your daily struggles, your daily 'grind'. That is when you need Him most.

O. HALLESBY

Have mercy on me, O God, according to Thy loving kindness; according unto the multitude of Thy tender mercies, blot out my transgressions. Wash me thoroughly from mine iniquity and cleanse me from my sin. For I acknowledge my transgressions, and my sin is ever before me. Psalm 51:1–3

Three

NEVER ALONE

'For each scene, I noticed two sets of footprints in the sand . . .'

Do you ever feel that you are carrying the world's problems all on your own? There are days when I feel just like that! There is a saying that a burden shared is a burden halved, but there are some problems that seem to double in size of their own accord, even when we are surrounded by family and friends. If we toss and turn in the early morning hours thinking about them, they become ten times as large!

I remember one such occasion when I received a telephone call from a cousin in California. She and her sister had visited us for a few weeks' vacation. Paul had not been well. I had mentioned that I was afraid Paul might take ill in the night, and I could never sleep well. One cousin (a missionary in India) had been observing Paul during her visit. When she went back to India she called her sister, greatly concerned that Paul might have diabetes. She sent a message that he should be checked for diabetes. Paul had recently learned that one of his closest friends who had diabetes had gone blind and just a couple of days before my cousin's call we had attended the funeral of a young man from our church who had died with diabetes. Paul had already had some tests but they had found nothing. Now, there would be a second test. I lay awake, imagining how difficult it was going to be to bear the burden of raising the children, earning an income, and caring for the home. The thought of being alone was overwhelming.

The next day, Paul was diagnosed with diabetes, but not with the extreme severity of all my fears. In fact, I said to the doctor, 'Oh, is that all that is wrong with him?' Out of that experience, I learned a valuable lesson I have not forgotten. Even when it seems the whole world has gone wrong, we are not entirely alone. There is a verse in the Bible that says just that. It is my favourite, tacked above my phone: 'Be still and know that I am God.' (Psalms 46:10)

All I needed to do during that restless night was to trust in God's loving presence. The prayers on the next pages remind us that wherever we go, we cannot step outside the boundaries of God's love and care for us.

Eternal Father, my crown on earth is in my heart, not on my head: not to be seen. My crown is called 'content'. This You have placed in me. It is a crown that seldom kings enjoy.

M. F. P.

Thou wilt keep him in perfect peace whose mind is stayed on Thee. Isaiah 26:3

My God and Father, while my footsteps tread the path far from my home, on life's rough way, oh teach me from my heart to say, Thy will O Lord be done! Renew my will from day to day. Blend it with Thine and take away all now that makes it hard to say 'in Your footsteps I must stay'.

CHARLOTTE ELLIOTT, 1881

Thy will be done on Earth, as it is in Heaven. Matthew 6:10

Father, I have wandered from Thee, often has my heart gone astray. Jesus, Thou art the Way, so I come leaning on Thy promises. Bring to me once again that joy that first I knew.

M. F. P.

Come unto me all ye that labour and are heavy laden. Matthew 11:28

Come Lord Jesus, fill my soul; That I may be in you made perfect and in every way whole. I am trusting, Lord in Thee, Blessed Lamb of Calvary. Before Thy cross I bow, Rose of Sharon, here I give my all to Thee.

P. L. P.

But God forbid that I should glory, save in the cross of our Lord Jesus Christ. Galatians 6:14

Lord, for tomorrow and its needs, I do not pray; But keep me, guide me, love me, Lord. Just for today.

SISTER M. XAVIER

As for me, I will call upon the Lord. Psalm 55:16

Thank you, Jesus, for Your promise to stay always with me throughout both good and bad times. Somehow in the good times, though, I don't see You, but only my own success. So challenge me today to see the difficult parts of my circumstances as an opportunity to feel Your steadfast love and faithfulness.

M. F. P.

. . . Lo, I am with you always, even unto the end of the world. Matthew 28:20

Take the world but give me Jesus,
Let me view His constant smile.
Then throughout my pilgrim journey
Light will cheer me all the while.

FANNY CROSBY, 1900

. . . Commit thy way unto the Lord; trust also in him . . . Psalm 37:5

O how sweet to walk in this pilgrim way. Leaning on the everlasting arms! O how bright the path grows from day to day, leaning on the everlasting arms of Jesus.

E. A. HOFFMAN, 1915

And it shall come to pass, that before they call, I will answer. Isaiah 65:24

Never a trial that He is not there.
Never a burden that He does not bear.
Never a sorrow that He does not share.
Moment by moment I'm under His care.

D. W. WHITTLE, 1893

. . . but the desire of the righteous shall be granted. Proverbs 10:24

'Tis the blessed hour of prayer, when my Saviour draws near,
With tender compassion His children to hear;
What a healing for the weary! O how sweet to be there!

FANNY CROSBY, 1903

Be still and know that I am God. Psalm 46:10

Christ, our Lord and Saviour, Oh be ever near me. Be our joy
throughout the day, Amen. Jesus hear us.

M. F. P.

*But seek ye first the kingdom of God and his righteousness; and all
these things shall be added unto you. Matthew 6:33*

Praise the Lord! for He is glorious; never shall His promise
   fail;
God hath made His saints victorious, sin and death shall not
   prevail.
Praise the Lord of our salvation! Hosts on high, His power
   proclaim;
Heaven and earth and all creation, laud and magnify His
   name.

FOUNDLING HOSPITAL COLL. 1796

Praise ye the Lord from the heavens. Psalm 148:1

Come, we that love the Lord, and let our joys be known;
Come join in song with sweet accord, and thus surround the
Throne, and thus surround the Throne.

ISAAC WATTS 1674–1748

Praise ye the Lord. Psalm 149:1

God is good, God is *good*, God is so *good*, He's so good to me.
He cares for me, He cares for me, He cares for me, He's so
good to me.

TRADITIONAL

Give thanks to the Lord, for He is good. 1 Chronicles 16:34

O God, our help in ages past, Our hope for years to come.
Be Thou are our guard while life shall last, and our eternal
home.

ISAAC WATTS 1674–1748

*Lord, Thou hast been our dwelling place in all generations. Psalm
90:1*

Four

GOD'S UNKNOWN WAYS

'. . . one belonging to me and one to my Lord.
When the last scene of my life shot before me
I looked back at the footprints in the sand
and to my surprise,
I noticed that many times along the path of my life
there was only one set of footprints . . .'

'In all the ways acknowledge Him and He will direct Thy path' (Psalm 37:3, 4, 5). I memorized this Bible verse many years ago, but I never really knew its meaning until one day in 1980.

We decided to move the family from Ontario, Canada to British Columbia, a distance of 4,500 kilometres, as we felt there would be more opportunities for our work with children. We were not even halfway there when we discovered that we had miscalculated our funds. Now, I will admit that we had stayed an extra night in the Banff Springs Hotel, mainly because a very special friend was working there, but, among other things, we were using far more fuel than we expected to need.

By the time we got to Roger's Pass in Alberta, there was some doubt in our minds as to whether this move was really God's direction at all. Funds were at an all-time low and, with four people sleeping and travelling in the van, things got a bit 'testy'. In the morning we stopped for breakfast at a café and decided to order two breakfasts to share between the four of us. As we held hands to pray, Paul shared with the children that we would have to cut back from then on, as we had to put so much more money into gas than we had anticipated. Our eldest daughter replied, 'Dad, if God is really leading us, He will provide for us.' We gave thanks and started to eat. What we didn't know was the family sitting opposite were watching us. There had evidently been many harsh and loud angry words on their holiday and the father was threatening to turn their motorhome around and go back home. They watched us for a while, and, although we kept our conversations very quiet, they must have overheard us discuss our finances and our expressions of faith in God. Eventually they got up and left the restaurant.

As we prepared to leave, the waitress at the desk told us our bill had been paid by a family who had sat near us. When we came out to the gas station the attendant asked us to come and fill the van with gas and a litre of oil. It had been paid for in advance!

These prayers help us to see some of the many unexpected ways in which God works behind the scenes of our daily lives.

Lord, I feel like a little child with my hand in Yours, being led by You through the darkness that makes up my life's path. I feel like I am stumbling and grumbling through the uncharted ways and I stubbornly want a map! But help me to remember that You have already seen the twists and turns of my life and that You know this is the best road I can take, while I hold Your hand.

P. M. P.

Shew me Thy ways, O Lord; teach me Thy paths. Psalm 25:4

O Christ in Thee my soul is found, found in Thee alone.
The peace and joy I sought so long, the bliss till now
  unknown.
Now none but Christ can satisfy, none other name for me.
There's love, and life and lasting joy, Lord Jesus, found in
  Thee.

(SOURCE UNKNOWN)

. . .we also joy in God through our Lord Jesus Christ, by whom we have now received the atonement. Romans 5:11

Jesus, I do trust Thee, trust Thee without doubt.
That whosoever comes to Thee Thou wilt not cast out.
Faithful is Thy promise, precious is Thy blood.
This my soul's salvation, Thou my Saviour God.
In Thy love confiding, I will seek Thy face.
Worship and adore for Thy wondrous grace.

M. WALKER, 1894

Far above . . . every name that is named. Ephesians 1:21

Leave me not, for I am lonely, dear Lord. The way I cannot
see; Lest I wander into danger, keep me, Saviour, near to
Thee. Leave me not, but let my footsteps ever follow after
Thee.

LIZZIE ASHBAUGH, 1889

*Thy Word is a lamp unto my feet, and a light unto my path. Psalm
119:105*

O Lord, Teach us to seek after the truth and enable us to gain
it; but grant that we may ever speak the truth in love; that
while we know earthly things, we may know Thee and be
known by Thee, through and in Thy Son, our Saviour, Jesus
Christ.

THOMAS ARNOLD 1795–1842

. . . this I know; for God is for me. Psalm 56:9

O Lord God, when Thou gives to thy servant to endeavour
any great matter, grant us also to know that it is not the
beginning, but in the continuing of the same to the end;
until it be thoroughly finished, which yields the true reward.

SIR FRANCIS DRAKE

*Humble yourselves in the sight of the Lord, and he shall lift you up.
James 4:10*

My Lord, you have led me here, within Your holiest place.
Here Yourself have led me with treasures of Your grace.
For You have freely given what earth could never buy.
The bread of life from heaven, that now I shall not want.

THOMAS KINGO, 1634–1703

*But it is good for me to draw near to God: I have put my trust in the
Lord God, that I may declare all Thy works. Psalm 73:28*

Have you met with grief and loss?
Are you overborne with care?
Do you faint beneath the cross?
Take it all to God in prayer.

H. H. PIERSON, 1919

Seek the Lord and His strength; seek His face continually.
1 Chronicles 16:11

Jesus is the sweetest name I know, and He's just the same as
   His lovely name,
That is the reason why I love Him so; Oh, Jesus is the
   sweetest name I know.

LELA LONG, 19TH CENTURY

Jesus Christ the same yesterday, and today, and for ever. Hebrews
13:8

The goal of prayer is the ear of God. The living child of God
never offers a prayer which pleases himself; he wonders that
God listens to him, and he accounts it a wonderful instance
of condescending mercy that such poor prayers as his should
ever reach the ears of the Lord God of Sabaoth.

C. H. SPURGEON

. . . neither His ear heavy, that it cannot hear. Isaiah 59:1

Dear Lord, I confess in agreement with the Holy Scriptures
that I am totally without excellence in the reflection of Your
Holiness. For this reason I am totally dependent on Your
inherited favour purchased so dearly on the cross.

M. F. P.

For by grace are ye saved through faith; and not of yourselves.
Ephesians 2:8

Precious Saviour, I am not only surprised at all of the most
wonderful things You have done for me since I think on
them so rarely, but, I am so embarrassed that I can be so
foolish as to not recognize the abundance of Your love which
grants me one good thing after another.

M. F. P.

But grow in the grace, and in knowledge of our Lord and Saviour
Jesus Christ. 2 Peter 3:18

Dear Lord, may my every thought be brought into full
captivity to the obedience of Christ, to accept Your ways
and the way You have chosen for me.

M. F. P.

. . . bringing into captivity every thought to the obedience of Christ.
2 Corinthians 10:5

Father in Heaven, You remind me in Your words that Your
thoughts are not my thoughts, neither are my ways Your
ways. May I be taught patience to wait and see, to trust and
believe that Your thoughts are best for me.

M. F. P.

God hath chosen the weak things of the world to confound the things which are mighty. 1 Corinthians 1:27

Our Father in Heaven, You have so graciously given us Your Son to redeem us. So many others have encouraged me to see You during the rugged path of my life. Use me, Saviour, to see the potential in others and to encourage them to become what You can make of them.

M. F. P.

By this we know that we love the children of God, when we love God, and keep his commandments. 1 John 5:1

Heavenly Father, Your Holy Word tells me to be strong and courageous, not to be afraid or to tremble at those who would come against You or me. Lord, You are God and the One who goes with me. You will not fail or forsake, even though I may not fully understand Your Way.

M. F. P.

He will not fail thee, nor forsake thee. Deuteronomy 31:6

Dear Lord, what a hope and comfort the scriptures give us, as we seem to walk blind, and unknown in surroundings that we know so well. The trust becomes stranded at times, as by faith we walk in Your unknown ways.

M. F. P.

. . . in every thing by prayer and supplication with thanksgiving let your requests be made known unto God. Philippians 4:6

Prayer itself is an art which only the Holy Spirit can teach us. He is the giver of all prayer. Pray for prayer – pray till you can pray. To learn prayer men must pray. The only place to learn prayer is in prayer, bent and broken on our knees. Prayer is skill developed through experience. Prayer, genuine prayer, has its price.

C.H.SPURGEON

I exhort, therefore, that . . . intercessions . . . be made for all men. 1 Timothy 2:1

Five

DEEP WATERS

*'I realized that this was at the lowest
and saddest times of my life.'*

Two months before our eldest daughter was born, Paul and I flew to Rochester, New York to conduct some meetings at Roberts Wesleyan College. We came back in a terrible snowstorm, and I was afraid my baby was going to be born on the flight. The stewardesses reassured me that they were well equipped to cope with such an eventuality. We had to fly into Buffalo and then take a bus up to Toronto, a total journey time of just under four hours.

The strain of travel put great stress on me, and I developed toxaemia, so the doctor suggested that I rest more. I took the train to stay with my mother and father for a short time. The night I returned to Toronto, my water broke and I was taken into hospital by Paul. After a week in labour, my beautiful daughter was born on 24 May (the Queen's birthday) – an unforgettable day. I was overjoyed, to say the least! Paul had immediate rapport with his gorgeous baby daughter. When I was moved to my room, I was just bubbling with pride and enthusiasm. I could hardly wait to share my news with an Italian girl in the next bed.

After chattering on and on about our beautiful, perfect baby with five perfect toes on absolutely perfect feet, and five straight slim fingers on each hand, I noticed she was smiling, but very quiet. Then I saw big tears streaming down her cheeks. I gently asked when they would be bringing her baby to her, and she sighed deeply and told me that her little boy didn't make it through the delivery. My heart sank and I felt such compassion. Each time the nurses brought my little girl to me, I felt such a strange sense of sadness and sobriety that I was unable to share the bundle of joy God had bestowed on me. I thought of Matthew 26:39, Jesus' prayer in the Garden of Gethsemane, '. . . not as I will, but as thou wilt.' Jesus knew how this bereft young girl was feeling; He too experienced sorrow of the deepest kind. The promise of Isaiah 42:3 is for all who have ever felt engulfed by grief, 'When thou passeth through the waters, I will be with thee; and through the rivers, they shall not overflow thee.'

Even when things seem hopeless or impossible, God can be trusted; in Christ, He faced suffering, desolation and death. No sorrow is too deep that He cannot feel it with us and no trial is so great that he cannot deliver us from it.

Master, the tempest is raging! The bellows are tossing high!
The sky is o'er shadowed with darkness. No shelter or help is
  nigh.
Carest Thou not that I perish? How cans't Thou lie asleep,
When each moment so madly is threatening a grave in the
  angry deep?

MISS M. A. BAKER, 1874

*And he arose, and rebuked the wind, and said unto the sea, Peace,
be still. And the wind ceased, and there was a great calm. Mark 4:39*

Lord, we pray not for tranquillity, nor that our tribulations
may cease; we pray for Thy spirit and Thy love, that thou
grant us strength and grace to overcome adversity. Amen.

GIROLAMO SAVONAROLA 1452–1498

The Lord is nigh unto all them that call upon Him. Psalm 145:18

What a friend we have in Jesus. All our sins and griefs to
  bear!
What a privilege to carry everything to Him in prayer:
O what peace we often forfeit, O what needless pain we bear.
All because we do not carry everything to God in prayer.

JOSEPH SCRIVEN 1819–1886

... him that cometh to me I will in no wise cast out. John 6:37

Father, I need Thee to teach me day by day, according to each day's needs. My ears are dull, so that I cannot hear Thy voice; my eyes are dim, so that I cannot see Thy signs. Thou alone cans't quicken my hearing, and purge my sight, cleanse and renew my heart. Teach me to sit at Thy feet, and hear Thy voice. Amen.

J. HENRY NEWMAN 1801–1890

Call unto Me, and I will answer thee. Jeremiah 33:3

Lord, help me live from day to day in such a self-forgetful way, that even when I kneel to pray, my prayers shall be for others.

C. C. MEIGS 1792–1869

Lord, Thou hast heard the desire of the humble: thou wilt prepare their heart. Psalm 10:17

O Father in Heaven, let me not live to be useless.

M. F. P.

. . . whatsoever ye shall ask in prayer, believing, ye shall receive. Matthew 21:22

Dear Jesus, there is some sorrow that seems too much to carry, there is some pain that seems too much to contain, and there are some needs that are too much to speak about. When the agony of life begins to crush me, where is Your promise of care, of comfort, of love? Where are You? Or is it perhaps that I have moved away from Your presence, Your comfort, Your love? Lord Jesus, direct me back by Your footsteps in peace.

P. M. P.

For my yoke is easy, and my burden is light. Matthew 11:30

Dear God, I would be true, for there are those who trust me. Father in Heaven, I would be pure, for there are those who care. Lord, I would be strong for there are those who suffer.

H. WALTERS, 1881

Strengthen ye the weak hands, and confirm the feeble knees. Isaiah 35:3

Christ be with me, Christ within me, Christ behind me, Christ before me, Christ beside me, Christ to comfort and restore me, Christ beneath me, Christ above me, Christ in quiet, Christ in danger.

ST PATRICK C.385–461

65

Whatsoever ye shall ask the Father in My name, He will give it you. John 16:23

Use me then, my Saviour, for whatever purpose, and in whatever way You may require. Here is my poor heart, an empty vessel; fill it with Your grace. Here is my sinful and troubled soul; quicken it and refresh it with Your love.

DWIGHT MOODY 1833–1899

. . . ye shall receive that your joy may be full. John 16:24

There may be heavy sorrows along my earthly way,
There is no dread 'tomorrow', but ever bright today.

A. A. PAYNE, 1907

. . . pray for one another, that ye may be healed. James 5:16

Lord, I'm pressing on the upward way, new heights I'm
  gaining every day;
Still praying as I'm onward bound, Lord plant my feet on
  High Ground.

J. OATMAN JR., 1891

Guide me, ever, Great Redeemer, pilgrim through this barren
  land.
I am weak, but You are mighty. Hold me with Your powerful
  Hand.
Bread of Heaven, feed me now and ever more.

WILLIAM WILLIAMS, 1717

*Moses gave you not that bread from heaven, but My Father giveth
you the true bread from heaven. John 6:32*

Lord, on You I cast my burden.
Sink it to the depths below.
Let me know Your gracious pardon.
Wash me, make me white as snow.
Let Your Spirit leave me never,
Make me only Yours forever.

JOHANN FRANCK, 1618

*You have cast my sins into the deepest sea, never to be remembered.
Malachi 7:19*

If your feet have lost the way, if your Star of Hope is dim,
There is One who hears you pray; go and tell it all to Him.

H. H. PIERSON, 1919

I will trust, and not be afraid. Isaiah 12:2

I will lift up mine eyes unto the hills, from whence cometh my help. My help cometh from the Lord, which made heaven and earth. He will not suffer Thy foot to be moved, He that keepeth thee will not slumber.

PSALM 121

Out of the depths have I cried unto Thee, O Lord. Lord hear my voice. Psalm 130:1–2

Tomorrow I plan to work, work, from early until late. In fact, I have so much to do that I shall spend the first three hours in prayer.

MARTIN LUTHER

In the morning will I direct my prayer unto Thee. Psalm 5:3

Thou art giving and forgiving, ever blessing, ever blest,
Well spring of the joy of living, ocean depth of happy rest!
Thou our Father, Christ our brother, all who live in love are
    Thine;
Teach us how to love each other, lift us to Thy joy divine.

HENRY VAN DYKE 1852–1933

Marvellous are Thy works; and that my soul knoweth right well. Psalm 139:14

Six

QUESTIONING GOD

*'This always bothered me
and I questioned the Lord
about my dilemma.'*

When we were only three years into our marriage and I was eight months' pregnant, Paul and I purchased a Christian film rental business from our friends, Bill and Rosie James, who were moving away. They were so good to us and left us various items of furniture and household equipment. Within two weeks we suffered a postal and transit strike. Almost immediately, our business came to a complete standstill.

After breakfast one morning, Paul left for the bus terminal to try to ship some orders. Meanwhile at home, I was praying. 'Lord,' I said, 'how could you possibly let us get into a new business, just to go broke? Especially when it seemed we were taking the right direction?'

But a tiny window of light opened on my heart that day, which caused me to fall on my knees and thank God for his provision. About mid-morning a knock came to the side door, and a large thick envelope fell through the letter box to the floor with a thud. I peeked out of the window and saw a scruffy, bearded man disappear down our front driveway. I opened the package and it contained a very large sum of cash. The brief note said, 'I am paying you back for a favour you did for me in saving my life. I have been "going straight" for five years, and have been saving a little every day'. It was signed, 'A friend, an ex-con.' The money carried us through for an entire nine months of difficult times of building up our business.

In everything, give thanks! Prayer often avails where everything else fails, and prayer is a necessity, not an option, for daily maintenance.

O Gracious God, on Thee I wait. With Thine own self my
being fill, as day by day my life I live to do Thy will, Thy
blessed will. To do Thy will, Lord, to follow where Thou dost
lead.

W. H. PIKE, 1905

Abide in Me, and I in you. John 15:4

Closer to Thee, My Saviour, draw me. Nor let me leave Thee
more. Pain would I feel Thine arms around me. I seek a
resting place. Closer with cords of love, draw me to Thyself.

E. E. CHAPMAN, 1912

And I will cause him to draw near . . . unto Me. Jeremiah 30:21

Does Jesus Care? Oh yes He cares.
I know He cares, His heart is touched with my grief;
When the days are weary, the long nights dreary,
I know my Saviour cares.

PHILIP BLISS 1838–1876

*I called upon the Lord in distress: the Lord answered me . . .
Psalm 118:5*

I don't mind questioning You Lord, and I know You don't mind me asking, challenging with a seeking heart. Because You know the answers, and because You are bigger than any question I can pose, I feel I can at least ask.

P. M. P.

Is there anything too hard for the Lord? Genesis 18:14

My heart has no desire to stay where doubts arise and fears dismay;
Tho' some may dwell where these abound, my prayer, my aim is higher ground. Lord plant my feet on higher ground.

J. OATMAN JR., 1881

In the day of my trouble I will call upon Thee: for thou wilt answer me. Psalm 86:7

Are there days when life is drear?
Days when faith and courage fail?
Turn to God who draws near;
Only prayer will aught avail.

H. H. PIERSON, 1919

. . . when thou prayest, enter into thy closet and when thou hast shut the door, pray to thy Father which is in secret . . . Matthew 6:6

Precious Saviour, I am weak, but Thou art strong. Strengthen me, my Saviour. Make me strong in the little suffering I have for a short season, for You know I am questioning this situation, but I also know that I must trust and depend upon Your Grace to get me through this day, and even through each hour.

M. F. P.

But the God of all grace, who hath called us into His eternal glory by Christ Jesus, after that ye have suffered a while, make you perfect, stablish, strengthen, settle you. 1 Peter 5:10

Loving Saviour, give me a new heart, O Lord, and accept me as a child in your school that I may learn all the lessons that You see are needed to fit me to serve You.

M. F. P.

Her ways are ways of pleasantness, and all her paths are peace. Proverbs 3:17

Our Father, there are times when strength fails me. Grant us divine power from day to day to follow in Your footsteps. Indeed, we ask for and expect the fulfilment of Jesus' promise.

M. F. P.

How much more shall your heavenly Father give the Holy Spirit to those that ask Him. Luke 11:13

If our petitions are in accordance with His will, and if we seek His glory in the asking, the answers will come in ways that will astonish us and fill our hearts with songs of thanksgiving.

J. K. MACLEAN

I will praise the name of God with a song. Psalm 69:30

I wonder sometimes if Your Word really means that I can throw the whole weight of my anxieties and frustrations on You? Do You really have a complete and personal concern for me, when there are so many others who need You more?

M. F. P.

Casting all your care upon Him. 1 Peter 5:7

Father, there is so much fading, transient glory, important today and forgotten tomorrow. Teach me the eternal, upside-down, inside-out values of Your kingdom. Help me, Lord, to make decisions today based on Your character, and as a result, share in some way in Your glory.

M. F. P.

76

The hour is come, that the Son of man should be glorified.
John 12:23

O God, I have so many doubts about myself, circumstances around me and my relationship with You. But I do believe You love me and want to help me. Lord, take that little faith and put it to work. I really need You.

M. F. P.

If ye have faith as a grain of mustard seed. Matthew 17:20

Father, Thank You for taking my faith, limited as it is, and making something of lasting value out of it. Help me believe that you care, You hear and You answer.

M. F .P.

Whosoever shall not receive the kingdom of God as a little child . . .
Luke 18:17

Seven

PROMISES THAT CANNOT FAIL!

*'Lord, you told me when I decided to follow You,
You would walk and talk with me all the way.'*

My mother taught me of God's love and promises from her knee. Every morning I would see her Bible and devotional book open on the kitchen table. She loved to pray, to attend church and prayer meetings. She taught her family the old hymns and choruses, and one favourite for me was (and still is):

'Trust and obey for there is no other way,
to be happy in Jesus, is to trust and obey.
When we walk with the Lord in the light of his Word . . .'

She always prayed faithfully for pastors and missionaries throughout the world. She never worried about what denominational group was sending them to the field for missionary work and their pictures were on display alongside family photographs. She sewed, quilted, rolled bandages, packed boxes for Christmas, birthdays and non-birthdays, as well as writing letters on a regular basis. It seemed we were always surrounded by missionaries who visited our home, and so it became natural for Paul and me to welcome missionaries in our home as our children grew up.

Missionaries have taught us many things about God's promises, and His protection. Even today, when I go to other countries, I shake out my shoes carefully before putting them on, and I pull back the covers of beds in case there are bugs or insects in the sheets. I check shower cubicles for scurrying scorpions and spiders. The only spiders I don't mind are the harmless huntsman spider of Australia or the friendly money spider of Britain! The rest turn me to jelly! Many times we neglect to thank God for His promises and His protection as He walks and talks with us each day, wherever we are, be it our own garden, or in the jungle, in the city or in the desert. These prayers celebrate God's watchfulness and care.

Wait, my soul, upon the Lord,
To His gracious promise flee.
Laying hold upon His word
As Thy days thy strength shall be.
Rock of Ages, I'm secure,
With Thy promise full and free.
Faithful, positive and sure,
As thy days, thy strength shall be.

W. F. LLOYD, 1879

In Thy presence is fulness of joy. Psalm 16:11

Grant, O our God, that we may know Thee, love Thee,
rejoice in Thee; and if in this life we cannot do these things
fully grant that we may at least progress in them from day to
day, for Christ's sake. Amen.

ST. ANSELM 1033–1109

If ye shall ask any thing in My Name, I will do it. John 14:14

O Lord, Thou knowest how busy I must be this day; if I
would forget Thee, O Lord, do Thou not forget me.

LORD ASTLEY 1579–1652

. . . I will answer him: I will be with him. Psalm 91:15

Grant me, O Lord to know what is worth knowing, to love
what is worth loving, to praise what delights You most; to
value what is precious in Your sight, to hate what is offensive
to You.

THOMAS À KEMPIS 1380–1471

. . . but the desire of the righteous shall be granted. Proverbs 10:24

Lord Jesus, I like to take Your promises out of context,
though I know it's wrong. I want Your promises to cater to
my needs, to satisfy my wants, to justify things the way I
want them to be. My way and not Your way, not the best
way. 'But You promised.' Your reply is, 'Read the fine print!
Finish the verse! Some blessings have a clause! Don't you
know I always answer, even if I pause!'

P. M. P.

*And we know that all things work together for good to them that
love God, to them who are the called according to His purpose.
Romans 8:28*

All the way my Saviour leads me,
Cheers each winding path I tread,
Gives me grace for every trial,
Feeds me with the living bread.

FANNY CROSBY, 1903

. . . when I cried Thou answeredst me. Psalm 138:3

Jesus will lead me night and day, Jesus will lead me all the
way, He is the truest Friend to me.

W. C. MARTIN, 1900

O Thou that hearest prayer. Psalm 65:2

God will take care of you, through every day, o'er all the
way. He will take care of you, God will take care of you.

CIVILLA D. MARTIN 1869–1948

I called upon the Lord in distress. Psalm 118:5

To do Thy will, yes, that is all;
To do Thy will, obey Thy call;
To follow, Lord, where Thou does lead,
To do Thy will is all I need.

W. H. PIKE, 1905

. . . and I will hearken unto You. Jeremiah 29:13

O blessed work for Jesus! O rest at Jesus' feet! There toil
seems pleasure. My wants are treasures and pain for Him is
sweet; Lord, if I may, I'll serve another day.

A. WARNER, 1898

. . . He is a rewarder of them that diligently seek Him. Hebrews 11:6

All my strength I draw from Jesus.
By His breath I live and move!
Even His very mind He gives me
And His faith, and life, and love.

A. B. SIMPSON 1891

*If any of you lack wisdom, let him ask of God . . . and it shall be
given him. James 1:5*

On the pathway as you journey,
There are hearts for you to cheer,
There is much for you to do in Jesus' name.
Don't fail His gospel to proclaim.

G. C. TULLAR 1912

The effectual prayer of a righteous man availeth much. James 5:16

86

Tho' the tempter may my path assail
I have no need to fear . . .
Against the hosts of sin
I shall prevail with Christ my King so near.

G. C. TULLAR 1912

He that followeth me shall not walk in darkness, but shall have the
light of life. John 8:12

Jesus, the very thought of Thee with sweetness fills my
    breast;
But sweeter far Thy face to see and in Thy presence rest.
O hope of every contrite heart, O joy of all the meek,
To those who fall, how kind Thou art! How good to those
    who seek!

BERNARD OF CLAIRVAUX 1091–1153

For consider Him that endured such contradiction of sinners against
himself, lest ye be wearied . . . Hebrews 12:3

Jesus, my Shepherd, Brother, Friend, my Prophet, Priest and
    King,
My Lord, my Life, my Way, my End, accept the praise I
    bring.
Dear Name! the rock on which I build, my Shield and Hiding
    place;

My never failing treasures, filled with boundless stores of
  grace!

JOHN NEWTON 1725–1807

. . . call upon the name of Jesus Christ our Lord . . .
1 Corinthians 1:2

The Christian life rooted in the secret place where God
meets and walks and talks with His own grows into such a
testimony of divine power that men will feel its influence
and be touched by the warmth of its love.

E. M. BOUNDS

He that dwelleth in the secret place of the most High shall abide
under the shadow of the Almighty. Psalm 91:1

Eight

FAITH AND DOUBT

'But I'm aware that during the most troublesome
times of my life there is only one set of footprints.
I just don't understand why, when I needed You most,
You leave me . . .'

I always prided myself on being able to find my way around any city or town throughout the world. Paul would just give me a map and I would head out, perhaps with one of my children as co-pilot in the passenger seat, and be certain of finding my destination with ease. I found that this sense of direction gave me great freedom and independence. Nevertheless, when we moved to British Columbia, I seemed to have great difficulty in finding my way anywhere and I had to put my faith in Paul and the map to take us across rivers and over winding mountain roads. Often, it all conflicted with my sense of where north, south, east and west lay. I could not understand it; navigating had previously been so easy.

Once, I was going to take a children's meeting in a town I had not visited before. My young daughters were with me and, as the afternoon wore on, I realized I was hopelessly lost, although Paul had given me clear directions. Evening fell and the girls became alarmed; they just wanted Daddy to come and find us. It was long past the time that the children's meeting was due to start so I gave up and parked in a motel car park which overlooked a busy highway. Suddenly, there was a horrible sound of crunching metal and glass as ten cars piled into each other below us. Sirens began wailing and, in my anxiety, I imagined Paul out searching for us and getting caught in an accident somewhere.

Just at that moment, miraculously, he drew up alongside us. 'Honey, are you all right? The church called me – I'll let them know I've found you.' Perhaps it's no surprise I was never invited back there!

That day I learned an important lesson. No matter how much faith we have in our abilities, they can let us down. It is far better to put our trust in God who watches over us and protects us. A similar incident happened in Washington state which made me give up boasting about my sense of direction for good! Instead, as I set off on a journey, I often pray one of these prayers.

You can have faith to move mountains, but how many mountains need moving? All I need just now, Lord, is faith to know that You can move them if I need them moved.

M. F. P.

If ye have faith as a grain of mustard seed . . . nothing shall be impossible unto you. Matthew 17:20

Thy love to me O God, not mine, O Lord, to Thee, can rid me of this dark doubt of unrest, and set my spirit free. I praise you, God of Grace. I trust Thy love and might. Lord you call me Yours, I call you mine. My God, my joy, my light. Thy love alone, my Saviour, can ease this weight of doubt. Thy blood alone, O Lamb of God, can give me peace within.

H. BONAR, 1879

And, having made peace through the blood of His Cross, by him to reconcile all things unto himself . . . Colossians 1:20

O Saviour, precious Saviour, whom yet unseen, we love.
O Name of might and favour, all other names above.
In Thee all fullness dwells, all grace and power divine;
The glory that excels, O Son of God, is Thine.

FRANCES HAVERGAL, 1881

Whom having not seen, ye love. 1 Peter 1:8

Almighty and most merciful Father, Creator and Preserver of Mankind, look down with pity upon my troubles. Strengthen my mind. Compose my bewilderment, calm my inquietude, and relieve my doubts, that if it please Thee I may run the race that is set before me with peace, patience, constancy and confidence.

SAMUEL JOHNSON 1709–1784

. . . when I cried out Thou answeredst me. Psalm 138:3

Through this changing world below lead me gently, gently as
  I go;
Trusting Thee, I cannot stray, I can never, never lose my way.

FANNY CROSBY, 1903

And they that know thy name will put their trust in Thee. Psalm 9:10

Heavenly Father, Who is our guide this night? Christ is the way, thro' Him alone can endless day and joy be known. Oh, Who is your Guide tonight?

CLEMENTS, 1906

Evening, and morning, and at noon will I pray, and cry aloud: and he shall hear my voice. Psalm 55:17

O Father, does my pathway always lead down life's valley with Jesus? He'll supply your every need, down life's valley with Him.

C. G. MAYNARD, 1915

We must through much tribulation enter the kingdom of God. Acts 14:22

I love the name of Him whose heart knows all my griefs and bears part; Who bids all anxious fears depart – I love the name of Jesus.

W. C. MARTIN, 1901

The Lord knoweth them that are His. 2 Timothy 2:19

Lord, increase our faith. We believe, help Thou our unbelief. Give us a true child's trust in Thee in all thy strength and goodness.

M. F. P.

Wait on the Lord; be of good courage, and He shall strengthen thine heart: wait, I say, on the Lord. Psalm 27:14

O Sheltering Heavenly Father, shadows may gather around me, as on my journey I go. Yet they can never confound me, sunshine will come soon, I know.

G. C. TULLAR, 1917

He giveth power to the faint; and to them that have no might He increases strength. Isaiah 40:29

You can do more than pray after you have prayed, but you cannot do more than pray until you have prayed.

A. J. GORDON

Behold, God is my salvation, I will trust, and not be afraid; for the Lord Jehovah is my strength and my song; . . . Praise the Lord, call upon his name . . . Isaiah 12:2,4

I have no help but Thine, nor do I need another arm to save. Then Thine to lean upon; It is enough, my Lord, enough indeed. My strength is in Thy might, Thy might alone.

HORATIUS BONAR 1808–1889

Thy face, Lord, will I seek. Psalm 27:8

Eternal God and Father, forgive me for my doubting the
work of Your Holy Spirit in my life. Grant that this day
will be the beginning of a renewed faith in Your constant
presence and the desire to use me as a tool of Your
great Love.

M. F. P.

*. . . seek the Lord thy God, thou shalt find Him, if thou seek Him
with all thy heart and with all thy soul. Deuteronomy 4:29*

My Father in Heaven, I praise You that the battle in life is
not given to the strong nor the race to the swift, for I am
neither. My desire is that I will be found among the true
and faithful to whom the victory is promised through Jesus
Christ my Lord.

M. F. P.

For sin shall not have dominion over you. Romans 6:14

Father, sometimes I stumble and have much difficulty
following my Saviour's footsteps. Show me Your grace which
can direct me and build me up to keep me close to You, until
the final day of inheritance.

M. F. P.

. . . I commend you to God, and to the word of His grace. Acts 20:32

I have resolved to pray more and pray always, to pray in all places where quietness inviteth, in the house, on the highway and on the street; and to know no street or passage in this city that may not witness that I have not forgotten God.

SIR THOMAS BROWNE

. . . He that keepeth thee will not slumber. Psalm 121:3

Nine

OVERWHELMED BY LOVE

'He whispered, "My precious child,
I love you and will never leave you . . ."'

Six years ago our daughter was involved in a serious accident and many are the times when I have felt great concern over her physical, emotional and spiritual health. But whenever I hit rock-bottom, I would be overwhelmed by a tangible sense of God's love and care. It felt like a warm wave washing over me, and His voice would come to me in a whisper, 'I love you and will never leave you.' As He breathed encouragement to me, I, in turn, was able to breathe encouragement that gave her strength to try to do things that she felt were not possible.

We have been so pleased to see God opening many new, and entirely different, avenues for her to minister to those around her. Although she can no longer do fine artwork, she is able to spend many fruitful hours making cross-stitch gifts for friends and relatives. Although she can no longer manage her large ventriloquist doll, she can very capably bring to life a small puppet doll, 'Jessica', in order to encourage hurt or lonely children. Although it is difficult for her to do her studies (which she once loved), she loves to read God's word. No matter the pain she feels, she always tries to be a pleasant, cheerful and helpful friend.

Against all the odds, we have seen our daughter's shattered hopes and ambitions rise to new life. This same overwhelming and powerful love raised Jesus from the dead and today it can bring resurrection joy to your heart.

The peace I have in You, my Lord, who pleads before the
  Throne of God.
The merit of Your precious blood, is more than tongue can
  tell.
The joy that comes when You are near.
The rest my Saviour gives, so free from fear.
The hope in You, dear Saviour, so bright and clear, is more
  than tongue can tell.

J. E. HALL, 1879

*And the Lord heard the voice of Elijah; and the soul of the child
came into Him again, and he revived. I Kings 17:22*

Thanks be to Thee, my Lord Jesus Christ. For all the benefits
which Thou has given me, may I know Thee more clearly,
love Thee more dearly and follow Thee more nearly, day by
day.

RICHARD OF CHICHESTER 1197–1253

Ask, and it shall be given you. Matthew 7:7–8

Cause us, Our Father, to lie down in peace, and rise again to enjoy life. Spread over us the covering of Your peace. Guide us with Your good counsel and save us for the sake of Your name. Blessed are You Lord, who spreads the shelter of peace over us.

PRAYER FROM THE JEWISH DAILY SERVICE.

For what great nation is there so great, who hath God so nigh unto them, as the Lord our God is in all things that we call upon Him for? Deuteronomy 4:7

My soul praises the Lord and my Spirit rejoices in God my Saviour, for He has been mindful of the humble state of His servant.

M. F. P.

And Mary said, 'My soul doth magnify the Lord.' Luke 1:46

O Lord, You know what is best for me. Let this or that be done, as You please. Give what You will, how much You will and when You will.

THOMAS À KEMPIS 1380–1471

In thee, O Lord, do I put my trust; let me never be ashamed: deliver me in thy righteousness. Psalm 31:1

Eternal Heavenly Father, I know the command 'Love your neighbour', but do You know my neighbours? Teach me to love my neighbours as a decision, not an emotion, so I can show Your love to the world, one neighbour at a time.

P. M. P.

. . . thou shalt love thy neighbour as thyself. Leviticus 19:18

Your love, precious Jesus, is the perfect example of how I am to love others, the perfect cannon, the perfect standard, the perfect love. How can I fathom a love that is so strong, so faithful, so unfailing? Help me today to show my love to You and Your love to others.

P. M. P.

For God so loved . . . the world, that He gave His only begotten Son. John 3:16

Though my weary steps may falter, and my soul a thirst may be gushing from the Rock before me, Lo! a Spring of Joy I see.

C. W. FRY, 1898

Let us therefore come boldly unto the throne of grace, that we may obtain mercy, and find grace to help in time of need. Hebrews 4:16

Thou my everlasting portion,
More than friend or life to me.
All along my pilgrim journey,
Saviour, let me walk with Thee.

FANNY CROSBY, 1903

The Lord is on my side. Psalm 118:6

Leave me not, for darkness gathers round about the path I
    tread;
Leave me not, but let my footsteps ever by Thy hand be led.

LIZZIE ASHBAUGH, 1889

*Let us therefore come boldly unto the throne of grace, that we
may . . . find grace to help in time of need. Hebrew 4:16*

Safe am I O Lord, if Thou dost guide me.
Trusting self, how soon I fall!
Walk life's rugged way beside me,
Thou, my Light, my life, my all.

F. E. BELDEN, 1886

*For thou art my lamp, O Lord: and the Lord will lighten my
darkness. 2 Samuel 22:29*

Lord, Saviour, never, never leave me, nor yet forsake me ere!
While I live by faith and do Thy blessed will: A wall of fire
about me, I've nothing now to fear.

C. W. FRY, 1898

. . . when thou walkest through the fire, thou shall not be burned.
Isaiah 43:2

Leave me not, for sin is near me; with temptation life is
    fraught;
Then through all life's toilsome journey, O my Saviour, leave
    me not.

LIZZIE ASHBAUGH 1889

And Isaiah the prophet cried unto the Lord: and He brought the
shadow ten degrees backward, by which it had gone down in the
dial of Ahaz. 2 Kings 20:11

Leave me not, for I am lonely, and the way I cannot see;
Lest I wander into danger, keep me, Saviour, near to Thee.

LIZZIE ASHBAUGH, 1889

Who shall separate us from the love of Christ? . . . nor height, nor
depth, nor any other creature . . . Romans 8:35, 39

He knows the way I take!
Whatever beside He's at my side and never will He forsake.
In joy or pain, in loss or gain,
He knows the way I take.

P. L. P.

Fear thou not, for I am with thee; be not dismayed, for I am thy God. Isaiah 41:10

My God, my Father, should friends forsake and comfort flee,
Thou God will keep me true;
There is a safe retreat for me, Yes God will keep me true.

W. C. MARTIN, 1916

Hold thou me up, and I shall be safe, and I will have respect unto Thy statutes continually. Psalm 119:117

Lord, I want to be more like You.
Someday the storm clouds will lighten, the tempest around
  me will cease,
Rainbows my skies will brighten, flooding my pathway with
  peace.

G. C. TULLAR, 1917

The eternal God is thy refuge, and underneath are the everlasting arms. Deuteronomy 33:27

With a purpose true each task pursue, just as He my
    footsteps lead . . .
Spreading far and near kind words of cheer,
Giving help to those in need.

G. C. TULLAR, 1912

O taste and see that the Lord is good: blessed is the man that trusteth
in Him. Psalm 34:8

We thank Thee, Lord God, Heavenly Father, for thy faithful
love and guidance. Teach us to receive Thy gifts so that with
grateful hearts we may enjoy the gifts which come from
Thee.

M. F. P.

I drew them with cords of a man, with bands of love. Hosea 11:4

Christ, the blessed One, gives to all,
Wonderful words of life;
Sinner list to the loving call, wonderful words of life.
All so freely given.
Beautiful words, wonderful words of life.

PHILIP BLISS 1838–1876

. . . the words that I speak unto you, they are spirit . . . John 6:63

Would you live for Jesus and be always pure and good?
Would you walk with Him within the narrow road? Would
you have Him bear you, carry every load? Let Him have His
way with Thee.

CYRUS NUSBAUM, 1861

As for God, His way is perfect. Psalm 18:30

Out of my shameful failure, Jesus I come.
Into the glorious gain of the cross, Jesus I come.
Out of earth's sorrow into Thy balm.
Out of life's storms and into Thy calm,
Out of distress to jubilant psalm, Jesus I come.

WILLIAM SLEEPER 1819–1904

*. . . He hath sent Me to bind up the brokenhearted, to proclaim
liberty to the captives, and the opening of the prison to them that
are bound. Isaiah 61:1*

God's object is to encourage faith and to make His children and servants see that they must take trouble to understand and rely upon the unspeakable greatness and omnipotence of God, so that they may take literally and in a childlike spirit His word: 'Unto Him who is able to do exceeding abundantly above all that we ask or think . . . be glory throughout all ages.'

ANDREW MURRAY

Whosoever shall not receive the Kingdom of God as a little child, he shall not enter therein. Mark 10:15

Ten

ULTIMATE HOPE

'. . . never, ever, during your trials and testings.
When you saw only one set of footprints
it was then that I carried you.'

It was around midnight when we had finished our prayer time, and we had been praying for our married daughter and son-in-law who had left earlier that day after a short stay with us. We had been expecting to hear from them about eight o'clock when they should have arrived home in the Okanagan Valley, in the mountains of British Columbia. Paul decided he couldn't wait any longer. Just as he picked up the phone to dial their number he heard their voices at the other end! There had been no telephone ring at our end of the line. They had just arrived and were about to telephone us, but the call connected without anyone dialling.

They related a testimony of God's saving presence. On the way, they had missed their regular turn-off for gas and refreshments. Their journey home takes four to five hours depending on road conditions. They had taken the next exit off the freeway, and had doubled back into a town called Hope. They found a gas station open, and stopped to get a fill-up. For some reason, despite being delayed, they mooched around the store, apparently wasting another fifteen to twenty minutes. When paying their bill, they heard on the emergency radio in the station a highway patrol announcement of a major snow and earth slide across the highway at the very place they would have been had they made their normal stop. An extra detour meant they arrived home tired and weary, but in one piece.

Knowing that my daughter and her husband were safely home, made me reflect on the setbacks and dangers that we encounter on our way to our heavenly home. As the verse of one of my favourite hymns, 'Amazing Grace', reminds us, we have a Guide who accompanies us every step of the way and who will welcome us home at last:

'Through many dangers,
toils and snares,
I have already come;
'tis grace has brought me safe thus far,
and grace will lead me home.'

JOHN NEWTON 1725–1807

Like a shepherd, Jesus will guard His children. In His arms
He carries them all day long.

FANNY CROSBY, 1903

*. . . no man is able to pluck them out of my Father's hand. John
10:29*

Oh, wondrous news of life and love!
That Jesus lives and reigns above!
He made the path to glory plain.
Oh, no! He did not die in vain!

F. A. BRECK, 1901

Faithful are the wounds of a friend. Proverbs 27:6

Cast on Him your burden you are too weak to bear.
He will give grace sufficient,
He will regard your prayer.

E. E. HEWITT, 1903

. . . without Me ye can do nothing. John 15:5

O Thou, the captain of my salvation, strengthen me inwardly and outwardly that I may be vigorous with spiritual purpose and disposed to every virtue with gallant undertaking. Be Thou pleased also to fortify my spirit so that I may meet life hopefully and be able to endure everything which Thou mayest be pleased to send me.

M. F. P.

. . . pour out your heart before Him; God is a refuge for us. Psalm 62:8

Knowing each step of my journey, better and brighter will
  be.
Clouds are rifted, life's burdens are lifted. I'm glad and free.

P. L. P.

Therefore if any man be in Christ, he is a new creature.
2 Corinthians 5:17

Oh, ye weary ones on the Path of Life,
He hath blessing rich for you;
Ye shall walk with Him and ye shall 'not faint'.
Hark! the promise ringeth true!

F. KIRKLAND, 1901

116

God shall supply all your need according to His riches in glory by Christ Jesus. Philippians 4:19

To the old rugged cross I will ever be true, its shame and
    reproach gladly bear;
Then He'll call me someday to my home far away, where His
    glory forever I'll share.

GEORGE BENNARD, 1913

. . . He humbled Himself, and became obedient unto death, even the death of the cross. Philippians 2:8

O for the wonderful love He has promised.
Promised for you and for me!
Though we have sinned, He has mercy and pardon,
Pardon for you and for me!
Earnestly, tenderly, Jesus is calling, calling for you and for
me!

WILL L. THOMPSON 1847–1909

Come unto Me, all ye that labour and are heavy laden . . . Matthew 11:28

Room and time now give to Jesus, soon will pass God's day
   of grace;
Soon your heart let cold and silent, and your Saviour's
   pleading cease.
Room for Jesus, King of Glory! Hasten now, His Word obey.
Bid Him enter while you may.

(SOURCE UNKNOWN)

*. . . behold, now is the accepted time; behold, now is the day of
salvation. 2 Corinthians 6:2*

O Jesus, my Saviour, with Thee I am blest.
My life and salvation, my joy and my rest;
Thy name be my theme and Thy love be my song;
Thy grace shall inspire both my heart and my tongue.

(SOURCE UNKNOWN)

I will love Thee, O Lord, my strength. Psalm 18:1

O send Thy spirit, Lord unto me, that He may touch my eyes
and make me see. Show me the truth concealed within Thy
word. And in Thy Book revealed I see the Lord. Amen.

MARY LATHBURY 1841–1913

All Scripture is given by inspiration of God. 2 Timothy 3:16

118

Oh use me, Lord, use even me, just as Thou wilt and when
and where;
Until Thy blessed face I see, Thy rest, Thy joy, Thy glory
share.

(SOURCE UNKNOWN)

*. . . this is the victory that overcometh the world, even our faith.
1 John 5:4*

Lord, You give me strength to do my work, grant that my
work be suited to my strength. While I live, let me live for
You; when I die, let me die in You. Living or dying, I am
Yours.

JOHN MASON NEALE 1818–1866

. . . He shall give thee the desires of thine heart. Psalm 37:4

O Lord, pour out Thy Spirit upon my soul! My will, my tem-
per, my tongue control; I want to be what Christ my Lord
commands and leave myself, my all in His dear hands.

M. F. P.

. . . before they call, I will answer. Isaiah 65:24

Teach us, Good Lord, to give and not to count the cost; to toil and not to seek for rest; to labour and to ask for no reward, save that of knowing that we do Thy will.

M. F. P.

If ye abide in me, and my words abide in you, ye shall ask what ye will, and it shall be done unto you. John 15:7

Lord, when my work on Earth is done and my new work in Heaven's begun, may I forget the crown I've won, while thinking still of others.

C. C. MEIGS 1792–1869

. . . the prayer of the upright is His delight. Proverbs 15:8

O Divine Master, grant that I may not so much seek to be consoled as to console, not so much to be understood as to understand, not so much to be loved, as to love; for it is in giving that we receive, it is in pardoning that we are pardoned, it is in dying, that we awake to eternal life.

FRANCIS OF ASSISI 1181–1226

. . . whatsoever ye shall ask in prayer, believing, ye shall receive. Matthew 21:22

Dear Father, sometimes I get so distracted by earthly things that I miss the point of being here on earth. Let me always remember that You are my ultimate hope and salvation, that You are the purpose of my existence.

P. M. P.

The Lord is my light and my salvation. Psalm 27:1

We hear His footsteps on the way! O work, while it is called today. Constrained by love, endured with power, O children, in this last, last hour!

LUDWIG VAN BEETHOVEN 1770–1827

. . . Eye hath not seen, nor ear heard, neither have entered into the heart of man, the things which God hath prepared for them that love Him. 1 Corinthians 2:9

From north to south Your children meet to lay their homage at His feet. All heaven and earth before Him fall and crown Him Lord of all.

DE FLUITER, 1915

If ye . . . know how to give good gifts unto your children, how much more shall your Father which is in heaven give good things to them that ask Him? Matthew 7:11

May He support us all the day long, till the shadows lengthen, and the evening comes, and the busy world is hushed, and the fever of life over, and our work is done. Then in His mercy, may He give us a safe lodging, and a holy rest, and peace at the last.

JOHN HENRY NEWMAN 1801–1890

This is my comfort in my affliction: for Thy word hath quickened me. Psalm 119:50

Ready for all Thy perfect will
My acts of love and faith repeat,
Till death thine endless mercies seal
And make the sacrifice complete.

CHARLES WESLEY 1707–1788

For we walk by faith, not by sight . . . 2 Corinthians 5:7

Changed from glory into glory
Till in heaven we take our place,
Till we cast our crowns before Thee,
Lost in wonder, love, and praise.

CHARLES WESLEY 1707–1788

O come, let us sing unto the Lord: let us make a joyful noise to the rock of our salvation. Let us come before his presence with thanksgiving, and make a joyful noise unto him with psalms.
Psalm 95: 1–2

Acknowledgements

Grateful acknowledgement is made to the following authors, publishers and other copyright holders for permission to reprint copyright material.

Bonar, Hartius, *When God's Children Suffer*, Kregel Publications, P.O. Box 2607, Grand Rapids, Michigan 49501–2607, USA

Bonhoeffer, Dietrich, *Christ the Centre*, HarperSanFrancisco, 1160 Battery Street, San Francisco, California 94111, USA

Bounds, E. M., *Bounds on Prayer*, Baker Book House, P.O. Box 6287, Grand Rapids, Michigan 49516–6287, USA

Hallesby, O., *Prayer*, Augsburg Fortress Publishers, P.O. Box 1209, Minneapolis, Minnesota 55440–1209, USA

MacLean, J.K., Source unknown

Murray, Andrew, *With Christ in School of Prayer*, Barbour and
Co. Inc., P.O. Box 110, Greensburg, Pennsylvania 07675,
USA